ELLA HICKSON

Ella Hickson's debut play *Eight* (Bedlam Theatre, Edinburgh) won a Fringe First Award, the Carol Tambor 'Best of Edinburgh' Award and was nominated for an Evening Standard Award. It transferred to the Trafalgar Studios, London, and PS122, New York. Her other plays include *Gift* (part of *Decade* for Headlong Theatre, St Katharine Docks, London); *Precious Little Talent* (Bedlam Theatre, Edinburgh and Trafalgar Studios, London); *Hot Mess* (Hawke & Hunter, Edinburgh and Latitude Festival); *Soup* (Òran Mór at Traverse Theatre, Edinburgh); *PMQ* (Theatre503 and HighTide Festival) and *Boys*. She completed a creative writing MA at the University of Edinburgh and spent a year working with the Traverse Theatre as their Emerging Playwright on Attachment. She has taken part in the Royal Court Invitation Group and is the Pearson Playwright in Residence for the Lyric Hammersmith.

Ella is under commission to Radio 4 and is participating in Channel 4's Screenwriting Course. She is a member of the Old Vic New Voices and has taken part in the 24 Hour Plays, Ignite and the T.S. Eliot UK/US Exchange.

Other Titles in this Series

Alecky Blythe
CRUISING
THE GIRLFRIEND EXPERIENCE
LONDON ROAD

Jez Butterworth
JERUSALEM
JEZ BUTTERWORTH PLAYS: ONE
MOJO
THE NIGHT HERON
PARLOUR SONG
THE WINTERLING

Caryl Churchill
BLUE HEART
CHURCHILL PLAYS: THREE
CHURCHILL PLAYS: FOUR
CHURCHILL: SHORTS
CLOUD NINE
A DREAM PLAY *after* Strindberg
DRUNK ENOUGH TO SAY
    I LOVE YOU?
FAR AWAY
HOTEL
ICECREAM
LIGHT SHINING IN
    BUCKINGHAMSHIRE
MAD FOREST
A NUMBER
SEVEN JEWISH CHILDREN
THE SKRIKER
THIS IS A CHAIR
THYESTES *after* Seneca
TRAPS

Stella Feehily
BANG BANG BANG
DREAMS OF VIOLENCE
DUCK
O GO MY MAN

debbie tucker green
BORN BAD
DIRTY BUTTERFLY
RANDOM
STONING MARY
TRADE & GENERATIONS
TRUTH AND RECONCILIATION

Ella Hickson
GIFT
PRECIOUS LITTLE TALENT
    & HOT MESS

Sam Holcroft
COCKROACH
DANCING BEARS
EDGAR & ANNABEL
PINK
WHILE YOU LIE

Lucy Kirkwood
BEAUTY AND THE BEAST
    with Katie Mitchell
BLOODY WIMMIN
HEDDA *after* Ibsen
IT FELT EMPTY WHEN THE
    HEART WENT AT FIRST BUT
    IT IS ALRIGHT NOW
TINDERBOX

Linda McLean
ANY GIVEN DAY
RIDDANCE
SHIMMER
STRANGERS, BABIES

Conor McPherson
DUBLIN CAROL
McPHERSON PLAYS: ONE
McPHERSON PLAYS: TWO
PORT AUTHORITY
THE SEAFARER
SHINING CITY
THE VEIL
THE WEIR

Chloë Moss
CHRISTMAS IS MILES AWAY
FATAL LIGHT
HOW LOVE IS SPELT
THE WAY HOME
THIS WIDE NIGHT

Elaine Murphy
LITTLE GEM

Joanna Murray Smith
BOMBSHELLS
THE FEMALE OF THE SPECIES
HONOUR

Ali Taylor
COTTON WOOL
OVERSPILL

Jack Thorne
2ND MAY 1997
BUNNY
STACY & FANNY AND FAGGOT
WHEN YOU CURE ME

Enda Walsh
BEDBOUND & MISTERMAN
DELIRIUM
DISCO PIGS
    & SUCKING DUBLIN
ENDA WALSH PLAYS: ONE
THE NEW ELECTRIC BALLROOM
PENELOPE
THE SMALL THINGS
THE WALWORTH FARCE

Ella Hickson

EIGHT

NICK HERN BOOKS
London
www.nickhernbooks.co.uk

A Nick Hern Book

Eight first published in Great Britain as a paperback original in 2009 by Nick Hern Books Limited, 14 Larden Road, London W3 7ST

Reprinted 2010 (twice), 2011 (twice), 2012

Cover image: Idil Sukan (www.idilsukan.com)
Cover design: Ned Hoste, 2H

Typeset by Nick Hern Books, London
Printed in Great Britain by CPI Antony Rowe, Chippenham, Wiltshire

A CIP catalogue record for this book is available from the British Library

ISBN   978 1 84842 059 5

Introduction

I created the characters of *Eight* in the hope of showing the effects, when taken to their extremes, of growing up in a world in which the central value system is based on an ethic of commercial, aesthetic and sexual excess. I, like my characters, am a twenty-something and have grown up in a world of plenty, unscathed by war or recession, a world defined by consumerist boom.

As far as I could see, the effect of such affluence was neither contentment nor discontent. It was, instead, wholesale apathy. In creating the characters of *Eight* I asked a group of twenty-somethings what they believed in – the almost unanimous answer was 'not very much'.

Eight, then, when it was written, aimed to show a generation that had lost the faculty of faith. These eight characters are societal refugees – who are struggling to muster belief in themselves or the world around them. The result is either apathy or, perhaps perversely, fundamentalism. Faith is a human impulse; if there is no outlet for it in mainstream society it can become warped and misguided.

A year has passed since I wrote this play and much has changed. What was then a whisper of recession is now an undeniable reality. The students I was writing for and about had little idea about what the job market would look like by the time they tried to enter it the following September.

The next few years for recent graduates are going to be extremely tough – *The Guardian* recently announced that up to 40,000 of this year's graduates will still be struggling to find work this September. Apathy is no longer going to be an option.

Whilst times will be hard – and I realise this may be easy to say when the worst is yet to come – I feel a little struggle may be no bad thing. For it's only when times get really tough that you work out what really matters – and maybe, by then, we'll be ready to believe in it.

Ella Hickson
July 2009

Premise

One of the central characteristics of the commercial world that *Eight* explores is 'choice culture'. From channel-surfing to Catch-Up TV and *X-Factor* voting – we are a choosy bunch, we get what we want when we want it. *Eight* reflects this in its set-up.

When I directed the first production of the play, I offered the audience short character descriptions of all eight characters before the play began. I then asked them to vote for the four characters whom they wanted to see. As the audience entered the auditorium, all eight characters were lined up across the front of the stage – but only the four characters with the highest number of votes would perform. The other four characters would remain onstage, reminding the audience that in each choice we make we are also choosing to leave something behind.

Such a process is not essential for a performance of *Eight* and directors, of course, should remain in control of the line-up and order of play if they should so wish.

Eight was first performed at Bedlam Theatre, Edinburgh, during the Edinburgh Festival Fringe, on 2 August 2008, with the following cast:

DANNY   Henry Peters
JUDE   Simon Ginty
ANDRÉ   Michael Whitham
BOBBY   Holly McLay
MONA   Alice Bonifacio
MILES   Solomon Mousley
MILLIE   Ishbel McFarlane
ASTRID   Gwendolen von Einsiedel

Director   Ella Hickson
Stage Construction   David Larking
Technical Director   Xander Macmillan

The production transferred to Performance Space 122, New York, as part of the COIL Festival, on 6 January 2009, and Trafalgar Studios, London, on 6 July 2009.

EIGHT

2

Characters

DANNY, *twenty-two*
JUDE, *eighteen*
ANDRÉ, *twenty-eight*
BOBBY, *twenty-two*
MONA, *eighteen*
MILES, *twenty-seven*
MILLIE, *thirty*
ASTRID, *twenty-four*

(BUTTONS, *mid-thirties*)

DANNY

*Danny is a well-built man in his early twenties. He sits on a
black box in the centre of the stage with a corpse's head lain
across his knee, he is feeding water to the corpse. He is wearing
jeans, a black wife-beater and black boots. Danny is twenty-two
years old but he appears much younger; his learnt manner is
one of faux aggression; however, he fails to disguise an under-
lying vulnerability. Danny is a little slow but essentially sweet.*

Danny, hushed, talks to the corpse.

Here you go, little one – head up, 'ave some water, come on,
your lips are all crackin', come on. Look, I can't be doin'
everyfing for you, it's 'ard enough sneakin' in for nights, that fat
bastard porter is gunna see me one a these days and I'll get
fuckin' nailed. Now come on, darlin'.

You're a nightmare, int you? I used to be the same. Mum
always said I was a pain in the neck, always bawling when she
was tryin' to get stuff done.

Danny walks forward and begins to address the audience.

Mum used to work for one of them poncey magazines; it's why
we had to move up north, to Preston; it's newest city in
England, you know? I was dead excited, shouldn't have been...
borin' as fuck here. Mum's job was to make sure all the people
on the front cover of the magazine looked right. I used to watch
her, it was like magic, she'd give 'em big old smiles and scrape
off all their fat, anything not perfect she'd jus' rub out, make it
disappear. When she was done all them people looked beautiful,
like, like – dolls. The problem was it made me sort a sad to look
at all the ugly people after that; all them people who look fat or
spotty or just sort a strange, when Mum made it seem real easy
to look just right.

At school, Hutton Grammar, I was never bright so sports were always my thing, and I was always big, like my dad has been. They used to call him Monster Cox, which I always thought was cos he was built like a tank but it turned out it was cos he had a massive dick. He died in the Falklands, he was a Sapper, part a the Royal Engineers, had a bit more up top than me. (*Laughs – self-deprecating.*) Mum always seemed a bit afraid after Dad had gone, she seemed sort a smaller, she didn't look 'right'. I guess that was why I wanted to get big, like Dad had been, to make things better – protect her, like.

I was sort of keen on goin' down the gym after school, cos it helped wiv rugby, and girls and that, so Mum, for my eighteenth birthday, bought me my first tub a protein shake, CNP Professional. At first it was just a hobby. I'd do, say, two hours after school, not much, like, reps of twelve – squats, crunches, lunges, flat-bench press, barbell curls – just the usual stuff. But it started feelin' really good.

I was feeling better and lookin' better, I can't remember which one came first – they sort of seemed like the same fing after a while. So I upped my hours. And yeah, there was pain but I could ignore it – I was focused like crazy; I felt I could do anything. I was like one a Mum's pictures, getting tighter and bigger and more and more perfect.

And soon it came. I could feel it. Sitting at the back of the classroom – I could feel my traps straining to get out a my school shirt, and all the girls were lookin' too, they could see that I was different, they could see the strength, the fearlessness – my body was proof of the size a my balls. I didn't need to be a hero, it was enough just to look like one.

But, but after a while people stopped lookin', and it didn't feel so good, it didn't feel right. I was still getting a bit bigger but the change wasn't as, as powerful as it was at the start so I started thinking all the same things again like why I didn't have a girlfriend, what the fuck was I going to do with my life and what Mum was going to do all on her own if I went 'n, 'n... It was like down the gym I'd felt perfect, unstoppable, and then suddenly nothing was perfect any more.

My dad always said, 'The more you sweat in training, the less you bleed in war.' (*Trying to be brave*.) So I signed up, 4th Battalion, Duke a Lancaster's Regiment, trainin' every Tuesday down Kimberley Barracks. We were the new boys; they called us Lancs in 4th Battalion, the babies. Hauled in one day 'n pretty much shipped out the next – direct service to Basra, unsure whether you had a single or return, that's what all the lads said. We didn't have a fucking clue what we were doing, but I wasn't bothered, I was there to fight – end of. I was pretty popular too; apparently it's quite comforting to have your arse covered by a lad built like a brick shithouse.

His vulnerability dissolves a little – his face hardens, suddenly he seems older, tougher.

'Bout halfway through my tour, the day came, the older squaddies had always said it; one thing'll happen, one day and you'll never be the same. Mine came, 24th June 2007, it was my twenty-second birthday. We're creepin' into some sleepy suburb, the Warrior tanks were following us up. Tension was up, the drivers were spiked, chewin' coffee granules 'til they dribbled black – but all was quiet – we were just having a nose about – (*Stops, stares at the audience*.) – I'm out front. (*Snaps head round*.) Suddenly, in bowls a fuckin' Yank Humvee – (*Danny jumps on top of the box*.) – they're chargin' through, all shouting 'GET SOME', pelting out bullets like it's a fuckin' fairground ride… my lot hit the deck thinking Jonny Jihad's out to play – (*He jumps down and hauls the corpse up in front of him as if it were a rubble barricade*.) – I'm squatting, low behind some rubble, waiting for the storm to pass when 'Booooom!'… There's smoke, I can hear screams but muffled, like, and… I'm down. (*He falls to the floor, begins to drag himself back up onto the box, panting, frightened*.) There's pain… in my left leg, those tosser yanks had woken a mean fuckin' beast, there were rag'ed Fundie Jundies runnin' fuckin' everywhere – I looked down and the whole of my left leg, hip to toe, skinless.

He is now back on top of the box, he stares down at his leg – he pauses, quiet, shivering.

It was like the bullets stopped, like there was silence. I stared. My leg was red and bloody, not a patch a skin on the thing – I could see all the muscles, workin', t... t... twitchin', all the ligaments – I couldn't even feel the pain. I touched it, it was soft and warm and huge, it was the most beautiful thing I had ever seen.

Then, suddenly the pain and the smell, the stink of burnin' flesh – I screamed – Aaaaaaaaah!

There was no way I was seeing service after that. Burns all over me leg, they took the skin from my arse and patched it together, scrape bits off, add bits on. It fuckin' fascinated me and as it healed, I, I missed it. It was like, seeing that, seeing how perfectly constructed I was beneath it all, I guess it was Dad's influence, the engineer in me – but I... I swear I'd never seen anything work so well. It was like suddenly all Mum's front covers, all those perfect men and women, they were nothing now, even getting ripped wasn't the same, the buzz is underneath the skin, that's where everything was right.

So I started workin' here. I'm a stripper... of bodies... dead ones. They ask me to peel back the skin, but careful like cos they use it for people with burns, like me. Then I slough off all the fat so they're ready when the medical students come in... (*He turns to the corpse.*) Shh, I know, it's horrid, don't worry little one. (*He puts his hands over her ears and hugs her to him, whispering.*) Medical students use 'em for their anatomy classes, it's not fair to talk 'bout it in front of them, though. (*Takes hands off.*) I work during the day, but then I hide whilst the porters swap shifts – when everyfing is dark, I creep out, it's awful quiet and somehow calm, like – and they're all lying there and I can just be with them, sitting a while.

I give 'em nicknames like all the squaddies used to do, like Dad was Monster Cox and I was Danny Boy, so over here we have Holey Joe, not because he's religious or anything but on account of the hole they left when they cut his pacemaker out, apparently they make the crematoriums explode and no one needs that at a funeral, eh? Then there's Bruiser, through there, cos he's a little banged up, I don't know why, something must a happened to him before he came in. He's like a father to me; he just listens and listens for hours.

And then here, here she is, this is Mouse, my little mouse, cos she's so small and fragile but so perfect-looking, I look after her real well, I never let her get cold or leave her on her own for too long, she gets lonely, like Mum did.

What it is, is that when someone is willing to sit with you, all exposed and vulnerable like they are, it makes you want to share, makes you tell 'em things you'd never tell anyone else. Cos they don't mind if you're big or strong or if people like ya, they'll listen anyway. And you listen right back… listen… hard… to that silence… beneath all the noise… and you can hear 'em… breathing, and quietly now… real quiet like, their hearts start to beat.

He climbs in next to the corpse on the box, places his head on her chest to hear her heart beat then lies down next to her and pulls her arm over him and drifts off to sleep.

Blackout.

JUDE

Jude is eighteen years old, dressed in school trousers, shirt and a tie. A large black block, centre stage, acts as a bed and a dinner table – navigated around in the opening sections.

This time last summer, Dad sent me to the South of France. The day I left, he stood on the front step and saluted my departure, like some bloody sergeant major, pair of baggy corduroys, copy of the *Guardian* wedged under his arm.

'Off you go, my son,' he yelled. 'You will walk away a boy and return a man!'

Except I could barely hear him cos he had Haydn's 'Farewell' Symphony booming out of every window. (*Moves to sit on block.*) When I stepped off the plane, the first thing I felt was the heat – it smacked me in the face, the stairs burned my feet through my shoes; I strained to see the city in the distance, but I couldn't see a thing, I was shitting myself.

Taxi dropped me off at Boulevard Victor Hugo. Now, my dad would have been in his element. I could hear his voice in my head: 'Did you know, Jude, that without Victor Hugo, I strongly doubt we would've ever had Dickens.' Really, Dad, that's fascinating. I felt for the sandwiches he'd put in the bottom of my bag, but I'd eaten them on the plane.

He starts moving behind the block, down a 'street'.

Twenty-three, twenty-four – fuck a duck… It was huge. Wrought-iron gates squeaked open, I carried my suitcase up to this big green door; the paint was all cracking off it in the heat. There were old-fashioned shutters and yellow walls. It looked like all the Riviera photos that Dad had showed me before I left, all those stories about – (*Sits, imitates Dad, talking down to imaginary Jude.*) – 'Fitzgerald, Picasso and Hemingway, when genius was valued, Jude, and the women, oh, the women,

beautiful muses with wild eyes and…' Oh, what did he say?…
Oh yeah, 'reckless abandon', as if he was a hundred years old
and he had been there himself – sad act.

I breathed in. I knocked. I was shown to my room by a crazy
and crooked-looking woman with fag breath who kept scowling
as my bag slammed against the stairs; 'Pardon,' I whispered
weakly, with this pathetic smile like I'd just peed myself.
(*Smiles.*) She growled – (*In a growly French accent.*) –
'Madame Clara will return later, little boy, for the dinner,'
alright. (*Sits on the side of his bed and looks around agog.*) As
much as I wanted to be back in Poynton, my French room
was… pretty fucking cool. The walls were covered in black-
and-white photos that looked like scenes from old movies and
that. There was a hat stand, here, in the corner – (*Imitates
popping his hat up onto it.*) – next to the bookshelf… busting
with crusty old novels, all in French, then my window… floor
to ceiling, old shutters that proper creaked and a balcony, little
radio, huge old mirror – it was brilliant.

*He flicks on the radio – Laura Fygi's Le Continental – he con-
tinues absentmindedly whilst dancing a bit and unpacking.*

Three months here might not be so bad, there was sun and sea
and there were bound to be women – (*He thinks.*) – in bikinis. I
was an independent man, my own room – I could be a Riviera
gent; look sharp, become fluent… in the language of looove…
eat well, get to know the place, maybe make friends with a…
baker. (*Jumps on block.*)

'Bonjour, Jude!'

'Bonjour, Pierre!'

'Say, Jude, where is that young lady I saw you with, eeh, she is
very good-looking, no?

'Eh, Pierre, she some needs some rest… from all the lovin'.'

I'm bloody hungry. What's that smell? It's like peppers or
something… this could actually be bloody brilliant… God, it's
hot, I need to get out of this stuff, I'm sweating *comme un
cochon* – (*Finds himself funny, starts taking off his shirt and*

shorts as he's dancing.) – and cologne, I'm definitely the kind of man that likes… colooogne – (*Imitates spraying.*) – mmm, the smell of that food…

He does a final twist, pretending to spray the perfume in his pants… He suddenly stops and the music cuts.

'Hello… um, um… p… pardon… Madame, Bon-bo-bonjour.'

His eyes hit floor, the same weak, 'peeing smile' continues, painfully embarrassed, humble…

(*To front.*) She was standing there, in the doorway; half woman – half silhouette. I glanced up, red nails and long, chocolate hair – blurry through the cigarette smoke.

(*Looks at his feet.*) I want to die, I want to die… I want to be wearing trousers.

Pause. One quick second glance.

Her cleavage, crinkly, brown – like a Sunday roast. (*Looks down at his crotch.*) Oh God, no, don't you dare, don't you dare make this any fucking worse –

He edges his hands over his… Looks up, smiles. He puts on a very strong accent, changes pose to imitate her.

'It's Jude, no?' she says… perfectly…

(*Gulps.*) 'Yes, oui, yes.' (*Clears throat in an overly manly way.*)

'Dinner is ready – in the kitchen, downstairs, you should – err – dress for dinner.'

'Yup, yes… yes, I should… I should, I will – thank you, pardon.'

Whilst re-dressing, he pulls trousers up from ankles, moves over to the kitchen, pulls out a chair – and nods recognition to imagined dinner guests.

The table was full of wine and strangers. Funny-sounding French and hands grabbing at massive bowls of food: salami and anchovies, little blobby tomatoes and fat balls of mozzarella, all swimming in thick oil, it smelled of basil and olives.

I took one olive – just the one. Clara looked down from the head of the table at me, '*C'est tout, Jude? Tch tch…*' (*Wags his finger.*) The two other lads, sitting opposite me, laughed. Jimmy on the left – a painfully stupid American who was absolutely, totally, incredibly excited about everything… always, and couldn't speak a fucking word of French – made me look pretty good. Then on the right we had Fabian, the quatri-lingual Bavarian; this scrotum-bursting, yak-haired, man-beast who kept having to pop off to play contact sports and plough wenches… twat.

It was a circus, controlled by the heavenly hostess, the red-lipped ringmaster. Not a piece of food passed her lips, she just quietly supped on red wine, and watched, smiling, as we gorged ourselves.

He moves over from the chair to the bed.

For the next three months, between language school in the morning and getting drunk in the evenings with Dipstick and Goliath, I spent my days sneaking glimpses of Clara. Her gold St Christopher twinkling in her cleavage over breakfast; wrinkled fingers dolloping handfuls of breast into expensive French lace. I had inhaled the heavy scent of woman. Perfection did exist, Dad had been right to have his idols. Clara Moretti, my Madonna.

Dad, in his absence, had finally come into his own. I had all this, this… urgh inside me, I couldn't sit still, I couldn't concentrate, there weren't enough wanking hours in the day. The only thing that made it any better was that little library Dad had packed me. I devoured every book, cover to cover. She became my aged Lady Chatterley, my jaded Juliet, my latter-day Anna Karenina, but I was just Quasimodo – looking longingly from afar, catching glimpses of her perfection whilst I remained this skinny, pasty and increasingly terrified teenager. It killed me; the more time I spent with her, the worse it was. I read books to her, I helped her cook, I watched her paint and all whilst she looked at me with sad and sympathetic eyes. She'd let me sit on the end of her bed when she got ready in the evenings – I'd fix the clasps on jewellery that glinted in the eyes of other men.

She wore her age differently with me, like it was heavy to carry, as if her skin was like an old friend that wouldn't let her forget a thing, not for a second.

As it got late, Mediterranean men would arrive in dark cars and wrap her in their heavy coats and they'd take her away from me; for those men, her age became like armour – I fucking hated those men for making her that way.

He takes his shirt off and lies on the bed.

At night, I could hear her fuck those Mediterranean monkeys, grunting and squealing as I lay, staring at the ceiling, sweaty and sleepless.

One night, Clara got a phone call at about ten. It was pouring with rain, the wind was furious, slapping the shutters back and forth against the walls. I could barely hear the conversation over the noise, but she was going out, to Monaco, for the night. I tried to sleep, I couldn't. It was so hot and humid, I paced my room, I smoked a bit. I was, I was… I had to walk, to breathe. I found myself outside her door. I pushed it open. The inner sanctum, without her in it; it was quiet, airy, the storm couldn't touch it.

He enters 'Clara's room' and sits on the bed.

Her white bed, the wooden floor, the tiny crystal bottles and trinkets sat gracefully and quietly, they were delicate, sophisticated, they aimed to tempt… one by one, the perfect crystal shattering, clouds of musk and powder flew up in my face. (*He chokes and backs away.*) Her lingerie, where *I* knew it was. Those perfect puckered legs wrapping around some fat Italian. (*He starts pulling at the stockings.*) Whore's stockings, black silk, all over her pure skin; expensive bras, made by a million hands, grubby little Parisian hands on her perfect body, holding her up and in… and – (*Runs back to her dressing table, mimics making-up.*) – pots of paint, the black soot in her eyes and the blood red on her lips, to paint the idol, as if she could get any more beautiful! Dad hadn't said it was like this! The lovers in his books – they were heroes, the passion of battle, he said – the honour of devotion, love makes a man but look at me – (*He sobs a little.*) – I'm fucking pathetic. I'm nothing... because she's everything.

He slides to the floor, sobbing, head in hands – he's young, vulnerable – quietly now, much more sombre.

And then she came back, she found me – in amongst her underwear. She stood above me, backlit by the street lamps on the road, her coat was wet, she said, she had to get dry – and her dress fell around her ankles, aging flesh creased and beautiful around her waist and down her thighs. She came towards me, lifted my face to hers and kissed me, hard; she asked me to hold her, to undress her – I did. And she was there, naked, all of her, to touch, to be had – she was above me, around me; she told me I was beautiful, angelic – she was human now. Her flesh between my hands, the weight of her, her perfume faded, there was just the smell of skin – her eyes pleading, the wet of her lips, her hands on me, I had her.

He wakes next to her, we see disgust in his face – the idol has fallen.

When I woke, the rain had stopped; the morning sun lay across her wooden floor and it crept into the creases around her eyes. She looked her age; too old to smell of wine and cigarettes, too old to have mascara down her face, too old for her lipstick to be smudged across the face of a seventeen-year-old boy.

Pause. He wipes his hand across his face, gets up and gets dressed back into school uniform. He stares out at the audience, something has been lost.

Blackout.

ANDRÉ

André, originally Andrew, is a twenty-eight-year-old gallery owner. He enters his gallery, clearly shaken, takes a moment to catch his breath and positions himself on a high stool.

I have to say, this wasn't the ending that I had in mind. I'm not sure what I did have in mind. Probably a whisper of a 'happy ever after', you know, wearing matching cardies, sharing digestives, but I hadn't thought I'd been stupid enough to pin anything on it actually happening. It's easy for the Cinderellas and Sleeping Beauties of this world, but we're a little low on route planners for Prince Charming and... Prince Charming. Serious lack of 'fairy' tales.

This certainly isn't one, is it? I think we can all agree that coming into work half an hour late on a Monday morning and finding your boyfriend hanging from the rafters by a Hermès scarf, well... it's not exactly 'happy ever after', is it?

That bloody scarf; I've always maintained that a high price means high quality but who knew Hermès could take a man's weight? And let's be clear, he was no skinny little fag, he was a big fat chunky. He was never going to wear it; I don't know what I was playing at giving it to him. He wasn't the scarf type, you see, Hermès or otherwise – never had been. I spent my teenage years trying my very hardest to look like Cyndi Lauper. Him? No, going with a button fly over a zip was his idea of outrageous.

Where's that sodding ambulance? He can't just be, up there, like that. I guess the rush isn't on once they know resuscitation heroics are out. More or less a removal job now – heavy load, lads, mind your backs. His big, purple face is dribbling all over an Emin print. Why he chose the bloody stockroom? It's not like he was being shy, putting a Hermès noose round your neck, it's not quite the same as popping a few pills and drifting off, is it? He might as well have done it in the front fucking window, nice bit of performance art... No, he wanted to save this one just for me, one-man show.

I bet I'm not insured for suicidal dribble either – that's 5k down the shitter.

They're bound to judge, aren't they, snoopy little paramedics? One art gallery, two queers, one corpse, that's never going to look good, is it? They'll look for syringes and... hamsters and expect some paid-by-the-hour twelve-year-old to pop out with a dummy in his gob. I wish we'd ever been that bloody exciting. He used to get a hard-on doing the tax return... seriously... it was the stationery, he said, the smell of fresh paper, straight-lines, colour-coding, gave him a buzz. He kept this place shipshape. It's our empire; Captain Admin and Sergeant Schmooze. It's all you need in the art world: a number-cruncher and someone that can talk bollocks at a million miles an hour, that's me.

He was never in it for the art. We caught the wave of the YBAs, you see, all that Hirst and Emin nonsense in the early nineties, when you could piss in a pot of formaldehyde and make a million, as long as you did it loud enough and in front of enough people. Dingy Hoxton warehouses and precocious teenagers sticking two fingers up at the establishment; like it had never been done before, like this time it might all crumble at the sight of their shit-for-brains art and polysyllabic waffle.

And all of them led by the grand high witch of overpriced nonsense... Miss Tracey Emin!

He turns and talks to Tracey Emin as if she is there.

'Now, Tracey dear, what you've done here with this little "bed" piece, is just not do your washing for a long while and what's happened is you've come off looking like a bit of a grubby slut, so come along, pumpkin, pop yourself in the shower and we'll get this tidied up.'

He really hated that Tracey Emin, and it took a lot for him to hate anyone; he said she looked selfish. I mentioned that might be because we were standing in front of a ten-foot photo of her scooping money into her lady garden. He said not, he said she had selfish eyes; that she was making tragedy a commodity and that was unforgivable.

You'd bloody love this, wouldn't you, Tracey darling...
'World's most boring man recovers old birthday present from flamboyant boyfriend and hangs himself with it' – wonder how she'd flog it? Something simple, get right to the core of it, probably some of those embroidered stick-men things – five grand a piece, for a game of Hangman.

He hated it, the drama, the hype – he tried not to, he read everything there was to read, he really felt that if people were paying all that money then there must be something in it that he couldn't see. Bless him. He always tried to see the good in things, invariably it wasn't there. See, it was never his world, it was mine.

I loved it, the parties, the glam, the feeling that you were getting away with it, free booze, free food, free drugs – people knowing your name. Recognition, it's short on the ground, you get it where you can. But he never needed it, not like me. I'd be raving my tits off in DayGlo and he'd have a pint and go home early, boring sod, didn't like the noise.

It was the same at the openings, print fairs, biennales – he'd lurk, he'd actually look at the art, whilst I schmoozed, made us contacts, did deals, showed my face, it's who you know not what you know, always has been, always will be. He never understood that, he felt that things should succeed on their own merit. Tch, tch... Not any more, love.

He never used his gayness either, and gayness is pretty serious ammunition in the art world. It's an indisputable qualification; gay men do aesthetics like black men can sprint, it's just fact. But he just didn't have very much gay in him. (*He raises his eyebrows.*) What I mean is, he was the least gay gay I'd ever met – well, excepting this recent episode, which, if he doesn't mind me saying so, is somewhat queeny. He drank Stella, hated gyms, never wore a pair of matching socks in his life, practically heterosexual. It was his niche: 'Totally normal bloke that happens to fuck men, please keep off the grass' – no cottaging, no arty wankers, no underage sex – go back to the nineties or see my seedy boyfriend if interested in any of the above. I was the yin to his yang, the Vivienne Westwood to his Marks & Spencer's, the St Tropez to his Bognor bloody Regis, and he needed me, I made him sure of who he was, by constantly reminding him of what he'd never be, what he'd never want to be. He was safe and sound on his patch, the only straight gay in the village.

Then all of a sudden, about two years ago, out of nowhere, he's overrun, in come the queers that aren't queer, they're getting married, they're wearing wellies and walking black Labs, they've got people carriers and kids instead of drug habits. The back alley had become memory lane and the sodomite became suburbanite. The poof had evaporated. These days being sub-versive is more of a hobby than a necessity. Even the names have changed – poof, queer, fairy, fudge-packer – they're not whispered or spat at you any more, they're hair products, club names, magazine titles, turn on the telly before work and watch Lorraine Kelly rubbing Poof in her hair.

So it all stopped, all changed, nothing left to hide or defend, why do it in the dark when it's all over bloody GMTV?

He hated it, how was he meant to tell himself apart? All that acceptance, you've never seen a man so lost – he had nowhere to go; he'd been sucked in, invaded, by normal.

Finally, Emin's getting old, that's where I got back from this morning, before… before this. I was at the National Gallery, twenty-year retrospectives start showing the wrinkles, love. Get a little bit of distance on it and it looks even more like bollocks than it did in the first place. If only he could've seen that. If he could've stepped outside of it all for long enough, got out of this place, got away from me, he would've seen that this isn't it, that this world of overpriced nonsense wouldn't win. I guess he couldn't see how it could be any other way; the faithlessness got to him, ate away from the inside.

I could see it happening, I watched him quietly shatter beneath it all. Sitting on the couch, eating himself into oblivion, there's more macaroni cheese in that corpse than I can bear to think about. But I didn't do anything. I told myself he knew, that deep down he could see, this world that I had brought him into, this shallow, shameless world of men with millions pandering to the tantrums of teenagers like Emin, of queers desperately trying to stay queer, I thought he could see it for what it was, see me for what I was, a joke.

But no, he thought we wanted more, he thought that if naked and dirty wasn't enough then it was time for paraplegic or post-op and he didn't want to see it, he didn't want to see me scrabbling around in the dirt for the last bits of different that were left, the not yet exploited; it was me; it was the fact I was still doing it, that's what he couldn't bear – if we could have both laughed at it from the sidelines, fine – but he thought I hadn't seen, he thought all of this, was me.

But what if I'd stepped down, if I'd stopped pretending… I couldn't carry him, I tried to get him down, lift him from the knees, I did, I had him in my arms, I took his weight for a second but he was too heavy. So I had to let go, let the Hermès take the strain. I stood there, watched his bloated, purple head loll forward – there was the shock factor, first time I'd felt it in a decade. And so perhaps this was his parting gift? To remind me of what it was like when people… stared, the thrill of shocking – how it had been when we were something to look at.

So this is it, the final fling for the queers at the fringes, the underground fairies… a little souvenir of when difference existed. And he thought this was what I wanted, what I missed? I would have given up the drama the day I met him, in all his beige glory. I've been bored of pushing the sodding envelope for half a decade, I just never thought to tell him, I thought he knew I was playing make-believe – but he didn't, I never told him that he, he was home.

Blackout.

BOBBY

*Bobby is a twenty-two-year-old mother of two – wearing a red
Adidas tracksuit. She is seated on a table. We imagine her kids,
Kyle and Chloë, four and six, at her feet in front of the telly.
She's reading down to them with enthusiasm. Bobby has a
strong, working-class Edinburgh accent, she mimics an upper-
middle-class English accent when impersonating Mrs Beeton.*

(*Reading.*) ''Twas the night afore Christmas, an' aw through the
hoose, no' a creature was stirrin', no' even a moose – '

Chloë, will you shut up and listen!

'The stockin's were hung by the chimney wi' care, in the hope
that St Nicholas soon wud be there.'

I know we dinnae hae a chimney, Chloë… but we do have a
lovely plasma-screen telly. We can hang our stockings b'that,
right? – Yes, Santa will know where to find 'em – They have so
got televisions in the North Pole… How else d'ye think Santa
got so fat if he wasnae watchin' telly aw the time, eh? Now
enough, you two, bed, now scram.

As (*imaginary*) *Chloë leaves, smaller Kyle turns around to
Bobby.*

Kyle, darling, what's wrong, wee man? Off you go with your
sister.

She pulls him up onto her knee, wipes his tears.

Big boy like you's no' scared of Santa, is he? What is it?
(*Listens to him.*) Oh darlin', I dae ken if yir dad's gonna be here
in the mornin'. Who knows, eh? But what I do know is that he
loves you very, very much and he's sent me the biggest, bestest
present in the world for you to open in the mornin'. But he
wrote me a wee note to say that you werenae to get it unless

you were in bed by twelve... there's that grin, go on – awa' you go, oot like a light – ye've got ten minutes afore I'm coming to check!

Bobby moves to behind a small table where she is packing stockings. She addresses the audience from here on in.

He's got them the biggest, bestest present in the world? What cack. That selfish cunt costs me double every fuckin' year, just makin' sure they dinnae realise what a pathetic shite he is. I'm too skint. I got caught by work, back in November; fiddling gift vouchers oot on the scheme. I was nicking the odd bundle, and sellin' 'em on for half the price, everyone's happy – 'cept Mr Tescos, o' course, he wasnae too pleased. Smug bitch in management caught me, gave me the push, three fuckin' weeks before Christmas. Is she havin' a laugh?

'Sorry, bairns, Christmas is cancelled this year!' Tch, as if.

I'd started thinking up some pretty scary ideas for makin' cash when I seen this advert in the local newsagent: 'Housewife seeks home help to aid in Christmas preparations.' Ten quid an hour, eight hours a week – brilliant. What the fuck kinda Christmas takes two people three weeks to prepare for, I dinnae ken, but I needed the cash.

This house, right – (*Whistles.*) – fuckin' mental! It was oot Corstorphine way, proper big-square number, fuck-off front door, little path, four windaes. It was like the pictures Kyle brings hame frae school. Actually, I dae ken why he's no' drawing concrete blocks wi' wee orange windaes? Mind you, he's still drawin' me an' his dad holdin' hands – so he's clearly an optimist.

The woman I was workin' for, her name was Mrs Beeton – she was really old and sweet, always makin' me cups of tea wi' these wee ginger biscuits. She had this big old family comin' up from London for Christmas, so she had to make puddings and cakes and pies but she was old, she got really tired, dead quick. I was sort o' glad I could gie her a hand. I thought it was a bit rough none o' her lot stayed tae help oot. They'd just come, stuff their faces and fuck off. She'd say, 'That's what mothers were for' – guess she's right. I don't think any of ma lot'll stick about once they're old enough to go… why would they?

She pulls her jumper in tight and heads over to the window.

It's getting cold. (*Looks out.*) Aw, would ye look at that? It's snowing – aw please stay till mornin', they'll love that.

There was this one afternoon at Mrs Beeton's, she called it 'Stir-up Sunday'. She'd come in frae walking the dogs. I was daen the ironin' in the kitchen, listening to *The Archers* – her choice, no' mine. I've got no patience wi' a bunch a twats that were getting fuckin' radgey over a duck. When oot o' her cupboards, no sort o' ceremony aboot it, Mrs Beeton starts pullin' bags an' bags o' currants, an' sultanas an' nuts and cherries an' all of it swimmin' in eggs. It was like Jamie Oliver's Christmas special but wi' a bit o class.

'Silent Night' slowly begins to play.

An' in her big old kitchen, fu' of heavy plates and heavy cutlery, and heavy old chairs and tables, wi' big orange lights an' wee little candles and her in her red apron, and her hair all pinned up, elegant-like. And she was playing these Christmas songs. Noo, we're no' talking Wham or Mariah Carey, or none o' that shite, this was a choir, and it was dead beautiful. And I watched her chuck aw this stuff in. She kent exactly what she was daen, like she'd been daen it for years, like it was some sort o' ritual.

Music down.

She asked me to grate an orange fir her. I felt stupit for gettin' sort o' excited, like a kid. Int that pathetic? Here I was, daen this old dear's ironing and peeling a fucking orange an' I could hardly contain masel. Life's no' that bad that some old dear's skiv work was going to make ma day; but it did… it really did. It was the smells. Oor Christmas, at hame, when I was a kid and Ma was aboot, it looked awright but it ne'er smelt a much, part frae Mum's fags and a wee wiff o' Iceland turkey. But the smell o' Mrs Beeton's kitchen! My God, I asked her what it was.

'Cloves, mostly,' she said. 'Cinnamon, your well-pithed orange of course, Bobby, a bit of brandy, nutmeg… sugar and spice and all things nice.' She laughed, she found hersel' quite funny quite a lot. She was sweet, though, there was nae agro to her, just sort of calm and quiet an' – just solid, ken?

As I was standing there aw misty-eyed, looking at her, wishin' I could take her hame and give her to ma kids for Christmas:

'Here you go, bairns, happy Christmas, have a better mum!'

She turns to me and says:

'Have you made your wish, Bobby?'

'Wish? Wish what?'

'Wish while you stir, dear. Oh, you have to wish, that's the whole point of it.'

'Oh right… Silly me, eh, forgot aboot ma wish, didn't I?'

Slower, softer, begins to cry.

So, I started makin' this wish about Christmas and my kids and… that… that… maybe it would be nice if we… maybe for once… could… (*To the audience, apologising for tears.*) – Sorry. I'm sorry. Like a stupit bloody kid maself I started cryin', and Mrs Beeton looked embarrassed, which is fair enough, what with her cleaner blubbing into her Christmas cake. She says:

'What on earth is the matter, dear?'

Through sniffles – getting progressively violent, building to a crescendo that is uncomfortably aggressive:

'I… I don't know,' I said to her. 'But it's just that it's Christmas and your hoose, it looks like Christmas and it feels safe and my flat disnae look like Christmas and it's never felt safe, no' for one single, fucking day and I don't know how to fix that, but I want to fix it, cos it's no' fair that my kids can't have what you have! Why can't they have a Christmas like this, eh? Wi' aw them smells, and carols, and the big old tree aw covered in twinkling shite an' everything that feels rock fucking solid.

What did you do, Mrs Beeton, that I never did, eh? Did you work harder? Cos I work fuckin' hard and I cannae make it like this. Or did you just have some good luck? Or, or maybe you just got given it aw an' you didnae dae a fuckin' thing!'

She'd backed her way into the armchair in the corner when I'd been shoutin'. She looked scairt, just a wee old lady, a wee old lady wi' me aw up in her face. There was silence, felt like hours o' it. And then slowly, I just sort of gave up.

Mrs Beeton pulled herself up oot the chair, and looked doon at me, this pathetic greetin' mess. I thought she was gonnae shout, or throw me oot but she just wiped her hands doon her apron, and said:

'Come along, Bobby; pull yourself together, these cakes won't make themselves.'

She drove me to the bus stop that night, she got out the car, an' handed me my things and said she'd see me the next day. No' even a whisper o' what had happened. As I was walking away, she caught my hand:

'If you must cry, Bobby, do it quietly, where they can't see you. Children are like animals – they can smell the fear on you. Plenty of people will show them real life. You, Bobby, you must give them magic. Birthdays, Christmas… it just has to be better than real, that's all.'

She hugged me. It felt like Mum, wrappin' me up in a towel, oot o' the bath when I was wee, aw warm and red and bubbly.

So this is it, I'm gonnae give them the best Christmas they've ever had. An' when they've got kids o' their ain they'll say, 'Aw, do it like Nan does, go on, do it like Nan does.' An' I'll hide wee treats for the bairns, and I'll make the biggest, bestest puddin's you've ever seen, and do you know what? You know what? It's going to smell great, fuckin' great. Just you wait, it's gonnae be magic.

Blackout.

MONA

Mona is a small, dark-haired girl in her late teens, with a mild pregnancy bump that is not seen immediately. Her hair is loose around her face; she has the innocence of youth and yet acts with disquieting intensity. The stage is set with a central block and one chair placed at its side.

She stands, quietly humming a child's nursery rhyme and climbs into the centre of the block.

This is the house that my mother built. This is the house that lets the outside in and keeps the inside out. There are no rules, no 'don't' or 'can't', no time to get up, no time to be home; just in and out, always in and out and everything always open. This is because when I was six, Mum discovered what Dad had done, what closed doors were really for – she called a builder man and told him to take all the doors away, every last one. The house became a big, toothless mouth, with gaping gaps where all the doors had been. Soon Mum found strangers to fill up all those gummy gaps. She filled the house right up with people, like grains of multicoloured sand; in they'd pour and out they'd run, rivers of funny-looking faces and brightly coloured clothes.

Mother has a hundred gods; she makes idols of them all – money, sex, beauty – she had the strongest, wildest laugh, as if nothing will ever matter ever again. She is the spoilt kind, the hair, the nails, the men, she takes what she wants. Nothing matters. She is, what you call… young.

Freedom, she said, that was my blessing. She said that I was part of the luckiest generation ever because girls like me had knowledge, and knowledge is freedom. My mother made sure that I knew all the truths before the world even began to speak to me. She made sure that I saw everything that there was to be seen.

But there was just one thing that was mine. (*She clambers to fetch the box, excited.*) A small box that I kept beneath my bed, for all the thoughts that hadn't been hers first; I'd whisper my secrets onto tiny pieces of paper and roll them into little balls, I'd blow them into the hole in the top of the box – (*Blow.*) – and plug my hand over it – (*Slap.*) – in case they ever grew legs and escaped. But they did escape, right out through the gaps where all the doors had been. Mother found my box and took it to her friends – they tipped out all my secrets, the tiny paper balls scurried across the table top searching for somewhere to hide, but there wasn't anywhere. Those Bohemians, with their red-wine mouths, laughed all my secrets right out loud. All the dark I'd ever had, all the dark that was mine, they pushed up into the light.

Mummy said that I was 'darling' and 'funny' and 'delicious' and 'odd' and that I was very silly for having secrets.

I ran away that day I…

Blackout. Someone approaches her, a young man with a hoody pulled over his head. He sits on the ground with his back to the block; she lies down, looking over him.

That was where I found you. You were slouched against a tombstone in the dark backyard of St Barnabus. You were strong and silent as if you were a thousand secrets stitched together into skin. I remember your body, bullish and defiant, even in the twilight. You picked me up, curly like a comma.

Music begins to play softly in the background. The boy rises and walks offstage.

I slept that night between the bright crimson walls of the room you gave me, the smell of incense up from the dim cloister below. There in the eaves, safe and sound – where I heard sermons in my sleep – (*She smiles rapturously.*) – there were doors, locks, keys, commandments – remember me, honour me, respect me, thou shalt not, thou shalt not – it was like sherbet on my tongue. You showed me the freedom found behind locked doors, the freedom of silence, never seen and barely tasted. Things there were firm and forbidden and I was found.

She pulls herself forward, writhing almost, sexual.

So there, in St Barnabas, I made a brand new box of secrets, I piped them in and plugged them shut, a new colony of thoughts... of you, and you never came to find them and you never poured them out.

On that last Sunday before they found me, you told me to wait for you, beneath the back arch, where all those concrete saints stared down at me in the cold. You stood a little way off, in a pool of street light. As you came closer, the width of your shoulders cast shadows across my face. I was humbled by your presence. You smiled down at me and asked if I was ready. You took my hand, I felt the scars on your palm press into my skin; those man-made life-lines that had made the gypsy scream, the fear in her funny black eyes, she'd never seen the likes of you. No one had.

The boy from before appears, hoody still up and approaches her. He travels with her back up onto the top of the block and sits beside her.

So I let you take me back to St Barnabas. It was colder now as the sun lowered behind scratchy black trees. I stared up at you, in awe, I listened to you and your silence; there was strength in your secrecy and yet you, the king of men, seemed a little vulnerable.

Mona removes the boy's top – we see a black crucifix tattooed onto his back. She climbs around him.

I clung to your back like a child; I ran my fingers down that black tattoo, across your shoulders and down your spine. You hadn't said a word when that little needle had thudded into your back, not a sound. And you were silent still but your breath was heavy, like a beast that knew his slaughter date was near.

The boy swings Mona over, onto her back and looms over her, the implication is sexually aggressive.

You roused and came above me, with eyes as black as death – dredging me – and then, unlocked me, like a door that had never been opened, by a master that knew the sanctity of what had remained hidden. To you and for you, I gave up my secrets, you didn't take from me, I gave you what was sacred.

The sun shattered into darkness and all was black. The beast in you was calm. I felt you slump against me, as you exhaled I felt your life in me, I was sacrosanct. I felt you heavy in my arms. You had chosen me to bear your weight, to stain, as your black blood ran inky over my clean, white palms.

They found me lying on the cold stone, with the sun just up – eyes wide open, where you had left me. Mother and her multi-coloured strangers brought me back to this doorless house where she and they and all the world cried and held me tight. They called you a million names; they found a thousand words for evil, a thousand new ways for telling this, the story of you.

They took me back to St Barnabus and found my box and tipped out all my secrets, all my thoughts of you, the tiny paper balls scurried across the table top searching for somewhere to hide, but there wasn't anywhere. Those Bohemians, with their red-wine mouths, read my secrets but they stayed silent now. No one laughed – I was no longer funny, delicious and odd.

You see, they fear the faith you've given me. They fear that I believe in you. And this, this is your testament, this is salvation. If only they would listen. But no, even this, they are taking from me now; they will take what is dark and push it up into the light. To them I am the dirty teenage child of a Bohemian. They think this is the price you pay for too much freedom. This is not a price to pay, the price has been paid, this is the only hope of redemption now. They will take this child from me and smite it because they no longer have the lungs for faith.

I have been returned to this boundless house, where laughing women break down doors and take what is not theirs; women, that steal childhoods from their children, so that they can wear a youth that is not their own. There is always a price to be paid for what we take; to open doors that should be shut, to take what is not freely given – it is not choice, it is not freedom, it is violation; you are gluttonous thieves, all of you. When you take, something must be lost, something breaks and someone some-where is left wanting. Don't let them take this from me, it is what he has given me to give the world, it is all I have, it is all you have.

Blackout.

MILES

Miles is an American man in his mid-twenties. He is dressed in a sharp suit and is attractive due to a corporate aesthetic. He should carry himself with ultimate bodily and vocal composure. The cracks in this composure should be perfectly synchronised with the glimpses of weakness in his performative façade.

Voiceover: 'This is the final call for all passengers to board flight BA293 to Washington. This is the final call, can all passengers proceed to Gate 13.'

Pause.

July 7th 2005, ten-second snapshot: a goofy young Asian guy is in front of me buying a Mars Bar, I'm in a drugstore, King's Cross Station, London. He turns to me, he's short ten pence, I give it to him. (*He mimes.*)

'Take it easy.'

It's early morning. I'm in a suit, I look down, I have slick shoes on. I walk out to the front of the station; it's summer, it's bright. I see the big white letters scroll across the top and I board a number 30 bus to Hackney Wick.

This is all that I have of that afternoon; snapshots, shards, flickers, facts.

Here's the facts: My name is Miles Cooper, born in Washington DC, 1982. I've won everything I've ever touched. At twenty-four I was the most successful broker Merrill Lynch had ever seen. I was the glory boy of the trading floor, making more money than I knew what to do with. My father was planning my biography before I was out of my teens; he always used to say to me, 'Miles, fifteen to fifty, make sure there's not a blank page – you're going to hit the top and keep on going, boy.' In April

2005 the DC office decided my skill was good enough to export, so I was going to London.

He sits, stares front – sinister.

Tick tick tick… boom.

I had lent Hasib Mir Hussain ten pence to buy a Mars Bar ten minutes before he boarded a bus to Hackney Wick and pressed detonate. He killed himself and thirteen other people that day. I, the one American on board, got out alive. I figure that would have pissed him off, right? Maybe he didn't catch the accent or maybe he was grateful for his final Mars Bar so he gave me some space.

I incurred some memory loss. Things broke up a little, fractured – so to speak. Everything from before the accident had a hard time holding together.

University College Hospital informed my family of my injuries and told them I would return stateside as soon as I was able. Merrill Lynch covered the cost, and I was booked to fly back to Dulles Airport, Washington DC, BA first class, August 2nd 2005.

My mother and my pregnant wife were waiting; they were excited to be having me home.

I think about Hasib Mir Hussain a lot. They printed his photo in the newspaper a week after the accident. I carry it in my pocket. He looked young, kinda dopey, he was lost. I remember his face when he asked me for the ten pence, he smiled at me. He didn't look like a murderer; he looked like a kid that was happy to have ten pence. He bit into that chocolate bar like a kid that knew it was the last chocolate bar he was ever going to taste. I'm glad I lent him that money. I owe him.

The night my flight left, I stayed in Heathrow Airport in a coffee shop; I just sat and watched the world walk past me. Everyone hiding behind newspapers or with music in their ears, eyes down and solitary but always acting like somebody was watching, performing, in their own tiny little music videos. I watched all those people, like a million little Charlies all hunting for the golden ticket, all desperate to believe that the chocolate factory still exists.

And then the sun rose, and I walked. I walked out of the departure lounge, out of Heathrow Airport, I walked onto a train, I walked out of Paddington Station, I walked through the city of London. That was the day I walked away.

He shifts from being dazed and controlled into a kind of commercial fever, choosing, spending, buying.

Eventually I walked into a tailor's. The guy asks me what kind of suit I wanted. I had no idea, I say, 'A suit like this one,' I say. I got three suits like this one. I walked into Starbucks, the guy asks what kind of coffee, I say, 'Coffee, just coffee.' 'Yeah but what kind?' he asks. 'I don't care,' I say, 'Just coffee.' I ordered a cab, I ordered a hotel room, 'Which room sir?'; I don't know, I don't care, it doesn't matter.

For the first six months following the explosion in Tavistock Square, I woke every day at 6 a.m., I ran for two hours, I showered, I dressed, I read the newspaper front to back and I was ready for my day. During those six months I stayed in fifteen different hotels, I fucked over two hundred women, consumed one hundred and sixty-seven grams of cocaine, and drank nearly two thousand units of alcohol. By December 31st 2006, I was nearly dead. During Christmas week the world had not afforded me any human interaction.

Early in the New Year, I started getting low on funds. I returned to Merrill Lynch and explained to them that the accident had led to my absence and necessitated my resignation. As I had hoped, I received a handsome golden handshake. I was speaking to my manager, Billy Driscoll. Fifteen floors up on King Edward Street:

'They want you home, Miles.'

'Sir.'

'I have a responsibility to tell them where you are.'

'Sir.'

'You know they think you are dead, Miles?'

Pause.

'Yes, sir.'

He didn't ring them. I don't know why. Maybe he thought they were better off without me, it would've been the first thing Billy Driscoll and I had ever agreed on. So I was dead. It was a year and a half since my accident and I'd finally died, I could stop running. If I was dead, I was free. Free of the suit, free of the wedding band, free of… free of fatherhood – I could do what the fuck I wanted – guilt-free.

After all you can't blame a guy for dying.

He punches the air, he's triumphant, crazed, he is possessed by the power of his freedom.

I felt like the elect! Like I'd been given a second bite of the cherry. I spent three months feeling and acting like a superhero. With Hasib Mir Hussain, Merrill Lynch and death as my bene-factors, I was loaded and liberated. I looked right, I talked right – I fucked right – I was the American all-star once again, but this time without any of the weight. I'd cheated the system. I fucked a lot, I drank a lot, I spent, a lot. Paris, Milan, Berlin, Tokyo – I ate the best food, drunk the best wine, stayed in the best hotels and people fucking loved me for it. They chose to be around me – men marvelled at me and women wanted me. Now, they couldn't have me because there was nothing to have but they didn't know that. To them, my inaccessibility was a mark of quality. They couldn't get what they wanted and women will always love you for that. It was so easy – onto yachts, into penthouses, into pussy – easy as fucking pie.

A break in pace.

And did I feel guilty? Did I feel guilty for the life I was leading – no. The actions of Hasib Mir Hussain on July 7th 2005 had made one thing very clear to me – that my existence was incidental. I had stayed alive because it had taken some time to get the change for my fare out of my pocket, because I had chosen to sit at the front and not the back of a bus; I had stayed alive because, having paid for his chocolate bar, I thought Hasib Mir Hussain might have wanted to make conversation and, frankly, I wasn't in the mood. I had stayed alive because I was an anti-social fuck. I was alive by chance and chance alone. Now, ask if I feel guilty – you show me the point of right and wrong when the difference between dead and alive is that tiny. What? You think I should be scared of not going to heaven? His or mine? Huh?

And the payback? The justice for walking away? For having spent my daughter's first birthday fucking a hooker called Lissi? For being that kind of man? There is none. If you agree to walk and you keep on walking – if you stay dead – it just disappears – conscience, guilt, bullshit – as long as you don't look back, easy as fucking pie.

But eventually you'll wonder, you'll wonder when it happened, on which day it became impossible for you to pick up a phone, on which day it was you could no longer walk through the door and take back what you gave away – you'll wonder when it became irreparable. And when you wonder you'll wonder yourself into the realisation that your escape has trapped you, and you'd kill for someone to give you an out, for someone to do something that justifies your behaviour.

As I said, I think about Hasib Mir Hussain a lot – I owe him.

Voiceover: 'This is the final call for passenger Cooper to board flight BA293 to Washington. This is the final call, can passenger Cooper go straight to Gate 13.'

Last week the Missing Persons Bureau received a call – Miles Cooper was staying in the Dorchester Hotel, London. The bomb blasts of July 7th 2005 had caused him retrograde and temporary antereograde memory loss – he called it global amnesia. Three years on and his memory had returned – he could remember snapshots, shards, flickers, facts.

Here's the facts. My name is Miles Cooper, born in Washington DC, 1982. I've won everything I've ever touched. My father used to say to me, 'Miles, fifteen to fifty, make sure there's not a blank page – you're going to hit the top and keep on going, boy.' On July 7th 2005 I had lent Hasib Mir Hussain ten pence to buy a chocolate bar, ten minutes before he boarded the bus to Hackney Wick and pressed detonate. I can now remember that I am a husband and a father, but unfortunately nothing else of the last three years – blank pages, so to speak. Today is my little girl's third birthday. I am flying home. My family will be happy to see me – easy as fucking pie.

Blackout.

MILLIE

Millie is an apparently well-to-do lady, in her early thirties, dressed in tennis whites and wielding a tennis racket. She is mid-mime, straddling an imaginary middle-aged man, flailing wildly...

She recites the first verse of John Betjeman's 'A Subaltern's Love Song'.

She smiles a motherly smile down at her 'tennis' partner and dismounts.

There we go, Robert, all done. Gosh, I always forget how much the old tetrameter really sets a pace, I'm puffed! (*Brushes herself down.*) Well, you better be getting back to your wife then – parents' evening tonight, isn't it? Well... luck to Amber and don't be beastly to her –

She turns and accidentally sees him in some sort of state of undress, and turns prudishly back to face forward, stumbling over her words.

– Oh, sorry, don't be beastly to her, I'm sure she's just creative rather than academic, we can't all go to – oh, you're done, excellent! If you could pop the cheque on the table by the door as usual and I'll see you Tuesday. Bye now! Bye bye.

She waves, smiling, until he leaves.

Robert Kendrick, lovely chap, massive fan of Betjeman, hats and slacks and fifties sensibilities. He hasn't dealt with the end of it all one little bit. Still longs for the soft twilight of a Surrey evening, cricket on warm afternoons, cardigans, and Pimm's. He's quite the old romantic, actually – (*Gets a cup of tea.*) – demands I recite Betjeman every time we 'have a cup of tea'. Robert shares Betjeman's passion for the robust lady – 'The strongly adorable tennis-girl's hand' – I try my best but I'm no

Sharapova. It's so difficult keeping the scansion straight with all that flailing, and when he demands I climax on those bloody dactyls, well, it's a tricky business, I can tell you. But Betjemen it is, he can't get enough of it. It's so hard for him, he despairs of his eldest, Amber, she's doing some sort of Gender Politics nonsense. He can't understand all that. No, Robert's education is more of the classical genre: Homer, Virgil, Plato – (*Pronounced with a hard 'g' and 'plah-toh' respectively.*) – who I always get mixed up with Pilates, but they're totally different. That's where we started, actually, with the classics. Then we tiptoed on up, through Donne, where we 'sucked on country pleasures', then a little raunchy Rochester, got very quickly bored by all those mild-mannered Victorians and ended up at Betjeman – blissfully short and comprehensible, really cuts down on a lot of bedtime reading. Very few people appreciate the kind of dedication that my line of business requires.

She looks at her watch.

Oop, listen to me gabble, only ten minutes 'til Thomas arrives, better start preparing those potatoes! It's Saturday morning, you see, busiest time of the week for me. It's ever since that *Saturday Morning Kitchen* lot set up, it's been tantamount to an invasion, suddenly Delia was off and that Antony Worrell Thompson was on. The results for my boys have been disastrous. Delia, Pru Leith, even good old Mrs Beeton in her day, they were role models, kept us girls on the straight and narrow – family values. But all these new Antony Worrell Thompson types have got wives across the country salivating over their slowly rising soufflés. You know what it is? It's all that feminism guff, it's led to such injustice. Along comes Nigella and – oop, televisions off, wives suddenly not interested. The minute their lovely hubbies want to indulge in a little gastro-porn of their own, it's unacceptable, disgusting even: 'Ooh, look at her, Jane,' they say. 'She's so gluttonous, so greedy, feeding her big fat face, oh look.'

Take my next client, Thomas Bishop, perfect example. He came to me last week and as he was having the little post-coital cry that he likes, do you know what he said to me, he said,

'Millie… do you know what?'

I said, 'No, Thomas… what?'

He said, 'I watched my wife orgasm last night, Millie.'

'Why, Thomas,' I said, 'Surely that's a good thing…?'

'To a Marks & Spencer's advert, Millie,' he said 'To a Marks & bloody Spencer's advert, just as all this cream cheese was oozing out of a burger… she squealed. I've never heard her make that noise before. And they're right, you know, Millie, this is not just food… this is adultery.'

Sad, isn't it? Watching it all fall apart like that. So I offer my services, I look after these lovely husbands, I take in the waifs and strays. I say, come one, come all. Come Rogers and Roberts, come Harrys and Humphreys, come to Millie Faucett-Reid's, she'll wipe your furrowed brow, press your shirt, serve a Sunday roast and offer a good, old-fashioned bonk, all within the hour. A traditional service at traditional prices.

Anyway, due to Thomas's new found 'gastronomic insecurity', his demands have become somewhat specific. Initially we thought we could combat the problem with a little role-play. If I became the food, he could triumph over me. Only, all we could find was a carrot outfit, and he had to sort of topple me into the bed, and penetration was a nightmare, so that ended quick-smart. Besides, he decided that to triumph over the food was not enough; if his wife lusted after grub, he must become said nosh. And there we had it, the breakthrough, he became the banger and I… let's just say I've had mashed potato in some very funny places.

Ooh, my tea! (*Runs back over to abandoned teacup.*) You see, absolutely everything is on the move for these men. Corduroys and a quiet country pub simply don't cut it any more. Women are being spoiled. They want new-age, new money, metrosexu-ality. My boys don't understand all that. Lovely Thomas wouldn't know a piece of pak choi if it boshed him in the face. No, my loafer-wearing warriors weren't made for yoga and tofu; they are men, soldiers, child soldiers, trained to make money and climb ruthlessly through what was once the glittering hierarchy of the British class system.

And then it came, the blackest of Wednesdays, the economic crash of '92. I was sixteen at the time, new to the profession, somewhat of a debutante, trained by my mother, but I could see what was happening, I could taste the terrible change in the air. I remember gasps and cries from my mother's bedroom, the tears of great men soaked her pillow that year. But as the economy crashed, FTSE falling... left, right and centre... my mother's takings soared. In they came, the soulless sound of a thousand wing-tipped brogues crossing the threshold. The day we pulled out of the ERM, my mother held the Right Honourable Sir John Major whilst he sobbed. He cried 3.4 billion tears that night. And that wasn't the worst of it: a thirteen-percent fall in the Conservative majority. Who can stand after that, I ask you? What man can hold his head high knowing that... Labour has got its grubby hands on power? They were done for, my Rogers and Roberts, my Harrys and Humphreys, finished. Oh, and it didn't take their wives long to philander: personal trainers, plumbers, mug-ugly football types – these were the men with money now, while my educated angels of the eighties, my proud boys, broken, faithless, unemployed.

So I came to my position with a passion for reinvigoration. Here, my boys could feel history, legitimacy and institution. My family have been in the industry of marital supplements for over five hundred years, we count Nell Gwyn amongst our own. And we're not going to stop now, no sir. 'We will not falter,' there, see, above the door, so they know, no matter what price is offered –

She stands to attention using the only salute she really knows, the Brownie salute.

I will never bed a Beckham
Nor bonk a barra boy,
The Faucett-Reids
Will mount their steeds
But never, ever the hoi-palloi!

She mimes spitting.

And I've been challenged on it too. Susie booked me a client last October, she does all my admin, I find it such a fiddle. Anyway, she let him past on account of his title, a title which, if you ask me, proves that even our dear old Queen can have an off day. I was all dressed up in my crimson corset, I usually find the aristocracy like a bit of bodice-ripping. So leg up, crop out, ready to receive my thoroughbred, when who should walk in the door but that bloody Alan Sugar! Oof – I was incensed! That four-foot-high, Furby-faced, epitome of everything that is wrong with this country. Predictably vulgar, he simply dropped his trousers and demanded a little 'how's your father'. Well, I firmly told him and his tic-tac to leave the building quick-smart.

She has already worked herself up and she tries to rein in this passion initially in the following lines, but it slowly builds until she cracks, revealing herself.

You see, we can't be doing with this… infiltration, this weakening. So much that is so beautiful will be lost. Everything, everything with meaning is under attack. My boys were once the best of British and now they're laughable – these are the chaps that made Britain great. Soon there won't be a Labrador or a welly in sight, then who'll be sorry, eh? I know I will. Let's keep our gentlemen, gentlemen, eh? Give them supper at eight, meat and two veg, let them play cricket at the weekend, I'd give anything to keep that alive, almost anything to be one of those wives.

She stumbles on the last word, repeating it, catching herself out, revealing too much. During the final line she composes herself, building up the mask again.

Come on, Millie, you silly old stick. Thomas'll be here soon. Better get those potatoes on the boil.

Blackout.

ASTRID

Astrid is in her early twenties. She is slim and attractive, the kind of girl that seems comfortable in her own skin. Tonight, however, she is a little drunk. She is returning from a night out and is dressed accordingly. There is a bed in the centre of the stage – the audience can see a man sleeping in it. She slowly climbs into bed next to the man – desperately trying not to wake him. She lies there, restless for several seconds, then sits up.

People talk about guilt as if it's an instinct. That the second you do something wrong, you feel guilty. I don't; what I'm feeling is power. You always join the story at the bit where they're sorry, when they're desperately begging for forgiveness; but there's something before that, there's now. In the space after the act and before the consequences, when you've got away with it; when you're walking out of an unknown door, back down unknown streets and it's still thumping in you – dawn's breaking, dew's settling and you're skipping back home, flying on the thrill of it, you can taste it. Even back here, the quiet click of the door, the tiptoe in – the alcohol's wearing off too quickly, I want it back – our bed and all the stuff that makes up life, our life – and – I don't feel like a traitor; I can lie here whilst another man's saliva dries off my lips and I can remember another man's face bearing over me – and I enjoy it, I enjoy that all this seems new again.

His alarm's going off in ten minutes. He'll roll over and grunt, curl himself round me like a monkey with its bloody mum. Just like every morning. He won't notice that anything's different – he won't see that I have mascara down my face or that my hair is wet, because I've been running in the rain to get back before he wakes up, he won't notice that I haven't been here, that I'm drunk, no – for him, I became invisible a long time ago.

She jumps up onto the bed and starts to inspect him, creeping around him as if he's an anthropological specimen.

That's not even snoring, is it? Listen? It's definitely more aggravating than breathing, but it doesn't quite have the conviction of a snore. Nope... just a slow dribble of air, as if it was engineered to be as aggravating as humanly possible; sort of like a tiny pony having a tantrum.

He sniffles slightly.

Oop – oh, that's nice, isn't it, a little wind from the baby. Having been with someone else, it's like I've left the room for the first time in years, and come back in and realised... this is the man that I once thought I might marry.

The man spreads himself across the whole bed; she jumps up and out of the way to avoid him.

Ah, and here we have – the spread. (*Mimics a wildlife programme presenter.*) Allowing air to all orifices at once, in vain hopes of ventilation, the male of the species spreads himself, much like a starfish, allowing little or no room for the female of the species to co-exist with him in the domestic habitat. It's as if she wasn't even there.

She shakes her head dismissively and climbs down.

It won't even occur to him that I could have done what I have. There could be all three of us in this bed and I still don't think it would cross his mind. That much trust... yesterday it made us strong, this morning it makes him weak.

Look at him. The sleep of the innocent, or ignorant... either way, it's bliss. For once I have him in my hands, ten minutes' time, he wakes up, and I make the call – I tell him or I don't tell him.

Let's say I tell him...

The sleeping man rouses and plays out the following scene in silence as she reacts.

He'll stare and gulp, breaths – big heavy breaths – then the anger will rise, he'll stand and it'll seem like something might break in him. (*He grabs her and roughly throws her onto a seat, she remains placid*.) And I will just sit, in silence – I'll squeeze my eyes shut and try not to hear him, because he might say some things that are true, about what kind of person this makes me, and I won't want to hear that. I don't want to see what I've done in his face.

The man puts his hand, softly now, under her chin and pulls her face round.

Then he'll make me look at him, and I'll remember how he can be soft – and he'll try to make me understand, to make me feel what he is feeling, realise how much I've ruined, but I won't. I won't feel what he will feel because I haven't had anything taken from me; what we've lost, I gave it away – but he, he's had it stolen from him.

The man gets back into bed.

But really, really what he'll feel, is a sense of thievery, and everything that I thought was soft and feeling will have been his ego speaking. He'll want to know, who the other man was, how big his dick was, if he was better in bed – this baffles me as a question. I mean, it's bold, isn't it, that, that 'Was he better than me?' I feel I want to offer some kind of recap, show him some clips of the last six months and then give him the chance to rethink the question. Here's the top three; him burping vindaloo on me as he ejaculated, the synchronisation was incredible, then there was me asking him to stop so I could remove his toenail clippings from beneath me because they were digging into my back, and finally the seven-pint impotence, Yeats had it spot on, it's like trying to stuff a muscle into a slot machine. And yet he'll still ask, 'Was he better than I am?' and if I respond honestly – 'Yes, Ben, he was much better in bed than you – it's barely even a contest…' then I'll be lying.

Break. She sits.

I've done the same – I've asked that question. I do remember how it feels – I remember being the unwitting victim. (*Softly approaches his sleeping head, says it to him:*) Sleeping quietly and faithfully, and then it's said or you just know – and then you're angry or more, desperate, to stop the moment when you accept your insignificance; when you realise that you were not enough. So you try to defend it, 'Was she better than I was? Hmm, bigger tits, eh?' and you realise you wouldn't be asking if the answer wasn't yes. And then? Then the visuals – you imagine him with her, the room, her cheap knickers on the floor, you like to think they're cheap – they're probably not, they are probably more expensive, more see-through, more size-eight than yours have ever been – and then you see his hands on her, his face in the moment that you are entirely forgotten. You wonder whether during the hour that he's fucking her, if you even crossed his mind – and you know you didn't.

She turns back to the sleeping man.

And you wonder whether during the past year and a half you even crossed his mind and you know you didn't.

But he – he was never entirely forgotten – no, no – I didn't forget him for a second. He was in every pant, and gasp, in every drink that got me drunk enough, drunk enough to want to see what it might take to make me visible. Such deliberate infidelity; it won't have been enough. Stay or go, tell him or don't tell him; to him it won't really make the slightest difference. Once you're invisible there's no way left to win, no buttons left to push. You see, the first one to stop loving has it – get left in the game and you're fucked.

She goes as if to leave the room, hesitates at the door and returns and climbs back into bed with the sleeping man.

Blackout.

Buttons was the first of these monologues to be written. It was
performed by Henry Peters at a scratch night called
Candlewasters at Bedlam Theatre, Edinburgh, early in 2008.

Buttons was left out of the final line-up of *Eight* because his
syndrome was too niche to appeal to the wide demographic at
the Fringe – he was a little too weird. I am, however, incredibly
fond and proud of this monologue; this ninth man, is, after all,
where it all began.

BUTTONS

*'Buttons' is a well-built, tensile-looking man in his mid-thirties,
grunting his way through press-ups on the floor of a prison cell.
The room contains a grubby campbed, a dilapidated toilet, a
desk and a chair. He will reach the end of a ten-year jail sen-
tence tomorrow morning. He knows the small space well, it fits
him and he owns it. There is a sense of latent sexual and physi-
cal power about the man.*

I often dream I'm a Victorian gent, suited and booted; top hat 'n
all. Head high, nose in the air, I'd 'ave those funny little white
things that fit just over the top a your shoes and with the nim-
blest of fingers I'd apply myself to the tiny spines of buttons
running up the sides of the clean, white material. Buttons…
them buttons, black, black buttons… patent, shining, glinting
into the beady little eyes of all them Victorian guttersnipes
that'd snatch at my feet as I swaggered past. I'd be dead good at
swaggering too, elite swaggerations, Captain Swagger, hung
like a horse; the kind a genitalia that makes a swagger a practi-
cal necessity rather than an aesthetic choice. Me 'ands stuffed

into those unfeasibly small, velvety little pockets, feet clacking, teeth glinting – and I'd be off to frequent a wenchsome establishment.

The wench, *my* wench, would be called… let me think, she'd be called – Ruby Tease. She'd love me… proper, unquenchable, salivating, lusty-type love, snatching at me, needing me all the time. Her feet would stay strapped tight into gripping, turgid little leather hooves of shoes, studded with those filthy little golden buttons, globular and glintin' – and – and – I'd rip 'em off, hold her fast and do her every which way. All those lovely Victorian ruffles scrunching in fistfuls… and she'd never stop smiling – cos she'd love me, proper love, cuddles-afterward love. She'd never make me pay; she'd just grin in a thank-you-very-much sort a way and I'd just walk away; free into my freedom, paying nothing and taking everything – magic, pure, human magic.

But then, when it's late and dark and I'm sitting here, deep into year three of this eight-by-ten grey igloo of an existence, and I'm so bored of staring at my own knob that I start to play, say, that game of… 'If my knob got trapped under a rock whilst out climbing in the Rockies, as I may well be of a day, and my only chance of survival was to lop the fucker off… how would I go about such a thing…?' I'm skirting through thoughts of penknives and razor-teethed racoons when all of a sudden, Ruby returns to my thoughts, only this time she ain't playing nice.

In this little ponderment, she's ripped the shiny black buttons right off a my shoes and they're glinting between her teeth… she's awfully angry, see. Her salivating, lusty-type love has turned to the incendiary kind, the kind that busts out a things, breaks doors, strains seams, scratches cheeks and draws blood, and I'm scared – I envision my Ruby's spitting fury and I know from the fire in her eyes that I have become the only man that matters to her – and so in my little Victorian, stuck-cock, dreamworld, I do the only thing I can do, the only thing that's kind; I smite her pretty little head against a wall, dash her brains. And all of a sudden-like, in my little cell-bound fantasy, my knob is free; I am free, out from under that colossal boulder.

But I ain't got no buttons on my shoes, I always went with Adidas Superstars – half-shell, not whole, greater flexibility for the all-star ducker and diver, see, but in 'ere they don't let you have the laces so I had to resort to the Stan Smith Velcro variety. I told 'em, I could just as easily top myself with Velcro, but they quite sensibly asked for a demonstration and truth be told, I came off lookin' a little silly.

I did get my way with the work-shirt situation though. When you enter the unit they issue you a costume of T-shirts, shirts and trousers – all having been inhabited by previous ne'er-do-wells, trusting, I suppose, that criminality ain't contagious. For transport into the unit they asked me to put on this work shirt, buttons straight up the front, the fiddly see-through-little-fuckers sort. I flipped my fucking lid – 'No way!' – I screamed and I kept screamin' 'til they brought the psych in. He had a kind old doctor face; said I was unusual but he'd seen it before, referred to my case notes. Sparky little number, he was; saw I wasn't lyin' soon enough, and I got to wear them beautiful button-free roundnecks for the rest of my stay at Her Majesty's pleasure.

I'm no freak, there are loadsa people out there with the same problem. You read stuff about folk getting nosebleeds when they touch 'em, or making their mates wear roundnecks on nights out cos the idea of a full-button shirt makes 'em vomit. I went to this group-therapy thing once just when it started; I was sixteen, I think. Mum made me go cos the lawyers had claimed my button phobia was at the root of my apparently aggressive disposition. I told the court it was a big bad 'four-holer' cut free of the granny's cardie that made me belt her round the head, nothing to do with her recently replenished pension book... But I must admit, in hindsight, it was probably a combination of the two.

This therapy shit was mental, it was sort of group hypnotism stuff, 'cept no one really got hypnotised, they were all just there with their massive made-up button phobias trying to get away from wives or parole officers. There was this one guy, Tobias; some joker sent to button therapy by his wife, he'd convinced her that he was so scared of the little buttony-munchkins that he had to stick 'em up his arse when he found one. Apparently that was the only place they couldn't get at him. But it was clear as day that his button therapy was more of 'I like it up the bum and I've got a wife' therapy, kinky fucker.

It angered me, you know, that the Tobiases of this world were just out for thrifty kinks and were using my very serious and troublesome disorder as some sort of excuse. I was for ever getting in scrapes because of it. Buttons just seem to sit on the sidelines of my life and just jump in, in all their terrifying discoid splendour, at moments when all I'd needed was a clear head. Just like with that granny, the free-falling freedom of three centimetres of circular plastic and suddenly I'm clockin' her round the noggin and stealing her bag.

Similar thing happened with a young Brazilian lady called Cildo, the very sound of which... as you can imagine... made me want to do the horridest things to her. Admittedly I was asking for trouble as she was part of my buttony-nutters therapy group. She invited me back to hers for a little after-hours therapy, all sweet and unassuming-like, I wasn't to know, really, was I. There I was, all de-boxered, standing to attention, gazing up at a ready-to-roll Cildo, when swift as a feckin' whippet, my new phobic friend opens the drawer of her bedside table, pops on a pair of latex and apparently button-resistant gloves, and starts pelting me, ten to the dozen, with all shapes and sizes of 'em, screaming, 'Dirty, nasty, wrong button-lover... dirty, nasty, wrong button-lover.' She'd been through a good ten repetitions and I had fucking awful bruising by the time I managed to re-boxer and get the fuck out of there. Nutjob, I tell ya, button nutjob.

You see, with behaviour like that, and with my heightened sense of anxiety due to my Johnson sitting there all vulnerable and eager, it's little wonder that I threw something back; admittedly it didn't have to be a bottle, and no I didn't have to smash it first, but it was close at hand and I was very angry. The buttons made me do it, I swear to you... they freak the shit out of me and they were *everywhere*. I needed to make her stop... and once she had, once she'd gone very, very quiet and all her thick, dark Brazilian hair just lay about her quiet head... then I was calm, and sorry, really calm and really sorry. You see, it's all sort of explicable, sort of understandable with just a little hind-sight and a comprehension of the mitigating circumstances... factor in a few buttons here and there, and suddenly I ain't so evil after all.

Tomorrow morning, having done my time in here for the granny and that bottle I stabbed into that filthy little buttony Cildo, I am walking free. I'll pop on my metaphorical top hat and velvety waistcoat, and stick my dirty little hands in the teeny little metaphorical pockets and clack my dapper shoes that glint their dazzling black leather, into the eyes of all the pokey grubbers at my feet. I will strut to see my Ruby Tease and clench fistfuls of her Victorian ruffles whilst I gruntingly exhale the pleasures of my freedom; and I hope I won't be back, stuck back in here with my cock under that rock again; cooped up and riled, tensile and angry... but I don't know. All depends, doesn't it? Buttons or no buttons, it's all about them buttons, I'm telling you – mitigating circumstances, psych said so – see, I ain't so evil.

Blackout.